W9-DGL-026

Bride's Little Book of

CUSTOMS
and
KEEPSAKES

CLARKSON POTTER / PUBLISHERS NEW YORK

acknowledgments

BRIDE'S especially wants to thank KATHY MULLINS, the books's writer and researcher, for the hours she spent immersing herself in the folklore of marriage. Many thanks to ANDREA FELD, BRIDE'S Managing Editor, for her invaluable contribution to the outline and content of the book, and for keeping the project on track. Heartfelt appreciation to ROCHELLE UDELL and MARY MAGUIRE of the Condé Nast Publications Inc. for making this book happen, to LAUREN SHAKELY of Clarkson N. Potter, and to BRIDE'S Art Director PHYLLIS RICHMOND COX. Applause to DONNA FERRARI, BRIDE'S Tabletop, Food and Wine Editor; RACHEL LEONARD, BRIDE'S Fashion Editor; and MARIA McBRIDE-MELLINGER, Contributing Editor, for originally styling many of the photographs in this book for publication in the magazine. Appreciation to staff member Mary Catherine McCooey, for arranging photographers' and other permissions, and to Denise Evans, for her computer wizardry. And, a very special thank you to all the talented photographers and professionals whose work appears in this book.

Photographers : William Abranowicz (pg. 19); Christopher Baker (pg. 34); Peter Bosch (pg. 44); Christopher Broadbent (pg. 14); Pascal Chevallier (pg. 12); J.R. Duran (pg. 26, top); Todd Eberle (pgs. 16, 17); Lee Friedman (pgs. 20, 21); Michael Grand (pg. 31); Douglas Keeve (pgs. 30, 32, 42, 43, 45); Paul Lange (pg. 29); Michael Mundy (pgs. 24, 27); Alan Richardson (cover; pgs. 4; 7; 8; 10; 18; 25; 26, bottom; 33; 38; 39; 41, all); Karl Stoecker (pg. 23); William Waldron (pgs. 22, 37); David White (pg. 35).

Additional Credits : Baker, Gail Watson, N.Y.C. (sugar boxes, pg. 4; floral wedding cake, pg. 10; favor cakes, pg. 38). Dresses, Bridal Originals (pg. 30); Ada Athanassiou for White Camelia (pg. 42). Favors, by Jan Kish, Columbus, OH (myrtle mini-wreaths, monogrammed mints, heart cakes, pg. 41). Flowers, Christopher Bassett, N.Y.C. (pg. 25); Blue Meadow Flowers, N.Y.C. (pgs. 8, 10, 33, 39); Bill Crinnigan, N.Y.C. (pg. 22). Hat-box design, Tom Thomas, N.Y.C. (pgs. 16, 17). Marriage certificates—Amish, by Ceci Good/The People's Place Gallery, Intercourse, PA (pg. 20); Quaker, by Harry Forrest, Cinnaminson, NJ (pg. 20); Persian, by Monir Farmanfarmaian, N.Y.C. (pg. 21); Jewish ketubahs (pg. 21), (left) Jonathan Kremer/Kesset Press, Ardmore, PA; (right) Ardyn Halter/Judaic Creations, N.Y.C. Porcelain swans, Lenox China (pg. 23).

Copyright © 1994 by The Condé Nast Publications Inc.
All rights reserved. No part of this book may be reproduced or transmitted in any form or by any means, electronic or mechanical, including photocopying, recording, or by any information storage and retrieval system, without permission in writing from the publisher.

Published by Clarkson N. Potter, Inc., 201 East 50th Street, New York, New York 10022. Member of the Crown Publishing Group. CLARKSON N. POTTER, POTTER and colophon are trademarks of Clarkson N. Potter, Inc. Random House, Inc. New York, Toronto, London, Sydney, Auckland.
Manufactured in Hong Kong.

Design by Justine Strasberg

Library of Congress Cataloging-in-Publication Data
Bride's little book of customs and keepsakes/by the editors of Bride's magazine.
  p. cm.
1. Weddings—U.S. 2. Marriage service—U.S. 3.Marriage customs and rights—U.S.
I. Bride's (The Condé Nast Publications Inc.)
II. Title: Little book of customs and keepsakes.
HQ745.B785 1994   93-25805
392'.5—dc20   CIP

ISBN 0-517-59679-2
10 9 8 7 6 5 4 3 2 1   First Edition

contents

introduction

Roots, heritage, ancestry...when we marry, these are among the things we hold dear. As wedding plans progress, the elements of our individual past begin to fuse with the promise of our collective future. Traditions, customs, even games open doors to history. The bride and groom who embrace these curious concepts become the richer for caring. "Honor thy family and all it symbolizes"— as we discover <u>why</u> the bride stands to the left of her groom; <u>why</u> she is veiled; <u>why</u> the wedding party carries flowers and always dresses alike. Keepsakes, too, deepen the meaning of this "Rite of Passage." The exquisitely embellished Marriage Certificate not only witnesses but enriches the occasion and the newlywed household. There is so much nostalgia here. This book of "Customs and Keepsakes" was designed to help celebrate our differences and applaud our similarities with new passion and understanding.

BARBARA TOBER

Editor-in-Chief, BRIDE'S magazine

betrothal

Romantic love—only in modern times has choosing a lifelong mate been left to love alone. Once, a bride was captured, bartered from a neighboring or royal family.

MATCHMAKING Seeking an astrologer or go-between for a successful match. Some Pakistani pairs are destined to marry when they are children. In Uganda, paternal elders barter for the family; in Arab countries, mothers scout the bathing beaches for their son's bride. A Malaysian mother presents the engagement ring to her son's fiancée.

THE BETROTHAL RING Asking for a woman's "hand in marriage" dates back to Roman times, when grooms traded a coin or a gold ring as a sign of security for the betrothal. In the Middle Ages, it was common to split a gold or silver coin and give half to the young woman and half to the man to bind their commitment. Since early Egyptian times, the circular shape of the wedding ring has symbolized unending love.

❋ THE DIAMOND RING Betrothal is sealed with something of value, often the diamond engagement ring, standard since fifteenth-century monarchs discovered its enduring qualities. Gemstones are also symbolic—amethyst (luck), emerald (youth), or ruby (safety).

❋ THE COURTSHIP RING Revive the posy-ring tradition. Poetic sentiments, such as "You and no other," are inscribed. Romantic Irishmen woo with a Claddagh ring — two hands clasping a heart —that dates back to the 1600s.

❋ LOVE TOKENS Victorians romanticized household objects — lace bobbins, pincushions, rolling pins were presented with all the sentiment of a valentine. Welsh men gave carved wooden spoons with heart motifs.

❋ WEDDING SPUNES Scottish bridegrooms purchased a silver teaspoon, called a Wedding Spune, which was engraved with the couple's initials and wedding date.

❋ THE DOWRY "His and her" expenses of yore were as formidable as reception expenses today. Marriage was a property exchange between families: The groom's family paid a brideprice (to compensate her family); hers bestowed a dowry to establish the young woman's household. The bride anticipated marriage, embroidering linens and lingerie, sewing beautiful bed linens and collecting them in an attractive hope chest built by her father.

betrothal gifts

In rural American communities, women stitch patterns, such as the "Double Wedding Ring," into quilts. ♥ In Germany, to mark their betrothed status, couples give each other plain gold bands that are worn on the left hand. They are referred to as bride and bridegroom throughout their engagement. ♥ Female relatives bestow status on Chinese brides with pocketbooks containing gold jewelry. ♥ Friends of American couples may stock their wine cellar, equip a home office, or chip in for matching luggage. ♥ An Iraqi suitor raises thousands of dollars for presents to his bride and her family. ♥ Africans value brides so highly that they give cattle, money, or labor in gratitude for a marriage. ♥ Members of the Navajo tribal community spin cotton to weave a fine blanket-like wedding garment for the bride to wear with pride.

❀ *Hope chest with household goods, treasured dreams.*

THE TROUSSEAU From the French word trousse, or bundle, the trousseau referred to the clothing and belongings the bride carried with her to her new home—sometimes heaped on a donkey cart for all to see. Today, it's all the new purchases and gifts for the marriage home.

THE SHOWER The bridal shower evolved as an alternative dowry. In Holland, a bride's disapproving father refused to contribute to her dowry, so supportive villagers "showered" her with household goods. Today "his and her" showers help the couple with everything from electronic gadgets to sporting goods.

THE BACHELOR PARTY The groom took the winnings from a last gambling fling — so he could still gamble once his wife had control of his money. After toasting the bride, goblets were smashed lest they be used for a less-worthy purpose.

THE SHIVAREE During the Middle Ages, a noisy band of friends banged on pots and shot off guns to disturb the lovers. The shivaree still embarrasses newlyweds in some rural areas of America.

Wedding-themed gift wrap can be as pretty as the present within.

WEDDING BANNS On three successive Sundays in the Catholic church, the impending wedding is posted in banns and announced so anyone can protest.

WEDDING PROGRAMS Guests can follow your ceremony, even when language, religion, or customs are unfamiliar. From photocopied sheet to a printed booklet, include the order of service, explanation of customs, words and source of readings, titles and lyrics of musical selections, translations, names of the participants. Add flair with artwork, ribbons, calligraphy.

SEATING CARDS Add decorative flowers, symbols to place cards. Names, table numbers should be handwritten.

wedding news

ANNOUNCEMENTS Tell your happy news to distant friends and family with formal printed wedding announcements that give names, date, and location of your wedding, in the mood and style of your invitations.

Keepsake invitation (left); sugar seating cards (above).

marriage certificates

THE AMISH FRAKTUR The fraktur designs created primarily by Amish and Mennonite artists are rich in symbolism. Crowned angels float atop wedding certificates and birds peck their chests to denote sacrificial love.

THE MARRIAGE CERTIFICATE Authentic nineteenth-century and modern versions of Quaker marriage certificates are available today. Both record family histories, vows, and leave room for guests to sign.

Folk art: Amish fraktur (above, left), Quaker certificate (above, right).

THE PERSIAN MARRIAGE CERTIFICATE An ornate wedding covenant...the modern interpretation of traditional Iranian certificates, decorated with birds, flowers, Iranian miniatures, Islamic symbols.

THE JEWISH KETUBAH A cherished art form, the ketubah is required for a valid Jewish marriage. Designs range from images that reflect a couple's interests to religious symbols or

Exquisite Persian keepsake (center); Jewish ketubahs (left and right).

depictions of Jerusalem. While the text originally detailed what the groom provided for the bride, many couples today opt for a ketubah that pledges equality in marriage.

The wedding party's clothes have always looked similar: The bride or groom might be kidnapped or harmed by evil spirits or jealous suitors. Identical attire kept ill-wishers confused.

superstitions

⊙ June weddings are lucky because of ties to Juno, Roman goddess of marriage and femininity. Sunshine is the luckiest weather, for the bride will be happy. If there is snow, the couple knows wealth; rain, no more tears. In Sweden, rain falling on the bride's wreath means the pair will prosper.

⊙ If an English bride meets a chimney sweep en route to the church, and he kisses her, it's good luck. He had a vital role in keeping home fires burning—safely.

⊙ Ducks join Korean wedding processions because, like many other fowl, they mate for life.

⊙ In Switzerland and Holland, a pine tree, symbol of fertility and luck, is planted at the newlyweds' home.

❧ *Swans, life-long mates (above); shoes herald a new family (left).*

wedding attire

❀ **THE WHITE GOWN** A bride wore her best dress, of whatever color, until 1840, when Queen Victoria's all-white gown with a Honiton-lace veil became fashionable. In Victorian times, white was a symbol of affluence and later, took on an aura of virginal purity. Now, white is again a symbol of celebration, as in Roman times.

❀ **THE COLORFUL GOWN** Brilliant red, signifying joy and love, is worn by Chinese brides. Indian and Nepalese

brides wear gold-threaded sarees and gold dust on their skin. An Amish bride sews a new navy-blue wedding dress. Icelandic brides may choose black velvet, embroidered with gold. Japanese brides change attire (the "color changes") many times during their weddings — from traditional white wedding kimonos to Western-style white wedding gowns, then colorful reception kimonos and ball gowns (in the bride's favorite color).

❀ *Most brides choose white.*

⚙ WEDDING FLOWERS Symbolizing fertility and everlasting love, flowers have long been a bridal tradition. Juno wore orange blossoms on her wedding night. Early aromatic nosegays of garlic, herbs, grains kept evil spirits away. In the "Language of Flowers," blossoms say "faithfulness" (ivy), "purity" (lily of the valley), or "true love" (rose). In India, both the bride and groom wear a floral headdress; in Hawaii, leis.

▩ *Camellias, tea roses, delphiniums, lilacs, azaleas, primroses .*

⚬ THE WEDDING HEADDRESS Long before delicate veiling was chosen for adornment in the sixteenth century, veils were worn by unmarried women as a sign of modesty; by married women to indicate submissiveness. Scandinavian brides marry wearing floral wreaths; Norwegian women, crowns decorated with silver bangles.

⚬ "SOMETHING OLD, SOMETHING NEW, SOMETHING BORROWED, SOMETHING BLUE..."

The traditional rhyme is still faithfully followed. Sew old lace in the hem. Wear a new string of pearls. Borrow a token from a happily married friend for luck; a blue garter or ribbon, for constancy. A lucky sixpence in the bride's shoe means bounty for bride and groom.

⚬ BRIDAL GLOVES Gloves are worn for fashion, modesty, and

romance. Victorians loved that without the "g" they were a pair of <u>loves</u>. A Greek bride puts a lump of sugar in her glove for a "sweet" marriage.

🌼 A BRIDAL HANDKERCHIEF A Belgian bride embroiders her initials on a linen handkerchief, which she carries during her wedding, then passes on to the next family bride. If she cries at her wedding, she'll never shed another tear in marriage. Many heirlooms are passed on, or created, at American weddings.

🌼 A LUCKY HORSESHOE British brides stitch a tiny horseshoe into the lining of their gown for good fortune; an Irish lass carries a silver horseshoe in the procession. From the days of antiquity, the U-shape was thought to protect against evil.

🌼 CHILD ATTENDANTS An adorably dressed child, carrying a flower basket or ring pillow, adds innocence to the wedding procession. Young Sri Lankan girls in white sarees sing "verses of blessing" and are given money by the groom. Spanish children present a silver box of gold coins to the groom, who shares it with his bride.

Friends gather at a Pakistani, Moroccan, or Indian bride's home before the wedding for a ceremony where hands, feet (sometimes arms, face, even hair) are colored in intricate, floral patterns with henna—for protection from unfriendly spirits. During this celebration, women sing wedding melodies and decorate the house with festive lights.

◉ In many parts of Africa, as well as in America, ceremonial marriage headdresses often include elaborate decorative braids. Some African

beauty rituals

brides wear their hair piled high in Goddess Queen N'zinga braids and may adorn them with red ocher dye.

◉ Some Finnish brides have their maiden braids cut off, then don a married woman's white linen cap.

◉ A Hopi bride and groom have their hair washed by their mothers before greeting the sun on their wedding day.

◉ Moroccans purify with pre-wedding milk baths.

◉ In Afghanistan, the exotic art of <u>zaraq</u> has been perfected over the centuries: The bride's face is adorned with colored spangles and gilt-paper strips.

◉ A Scottish bridegroom has his feet bathed on the evening before his wedding.

THE GIVING AWAY Brides today are escorted to the altar by their fathers, or "significant persons," but are rarely given away, a custom tied to arranged marriages, when the bride was property. The officiant may ask instead, "Who supports this man and this woman?"

ceremony rites

ALTAR POSITION The bride stands to the groom's left, a remnant of marriage by capture, when he needed his sword hand free for defense.

CIRCLES OF LOVE An Indian Sikh couple circle six times, then are showered with rose petals, to ward off evil on life's long journey. Greek couples circle the altar three times, for the Holy Trinity.

TYING THE KNOT Mexican couples are bound in marriage with a long rosary.

FOOD AND WINE Navajo couples taste pudding made by their parents, a sharing of domestic life. Japanese pairs sip three times from three cups of sake; three and nine are lucky numbers.

The bride is escorted to the altar (left); ceremonial sterling cup for Jewish wedding wine (right).

⚜ THE HUPPAH Jewish couples stand under an ornamental canopy of flowers or handpainted or embroidered silk cloth to symbolize the nomadic tents of Israel and the new home they will share.

⚜ BREAKING THE GLASS Jewish grooms smash a glass with their foot to remember the destruction of the temple in Jerusalem and that sorrow always tempers joy. Couples may preserve the shards in a symbolic keepsake box.

⚜ THE UNITY CANDLE The single Unity Candle is lit with two individual family tapers. This is not unlike the South African !Kung ceremony in which both sets of parents carry fire from their own hearths to start a fire for the newlyweds' home.

⚜ THE KISS From early Roman times, it was a legal bond that sealed contracts. Once, an engagement was null without one. Many euphoric pairs share their joy by including the Kiss of Peace — a hug or handshake passed from clergymember and the couple to attendants and guests.

❖ *A flower-trimmed Unity candle (above); a romantic huppah (right).*

Wedding processions wind through French villages. Joyous parades to reception sites, led by jazz musicians and maids carrying decorated umbrellas, are common in Louisiana. After an Egyptian ceremony, the revelry is led by belly dancers, men with flaming swords and horns.

processions

⊛ A BRIDAL PATH strewn with rose petals might ward off evil spirits below ground and grant fertility, a wished-for bridal virtue. White aisle runners secure her safety, too.

⊛ AN ARCH OF SWORDS OR SABERS by a military honor guard grants the departing newlyweds safe passage. For fun: golf clubs, oars.

⊛ THE RECEIVING LINE is a convenient way to greet each guest. Chinese couples toast at each table to pay respect. Indonesians greet their many guests twice (each guest is a blessing).

⊛ JUMPING THE BROOM, a public marriage commitment for generations of slaves forbidden legal or religious rites, symbolizes new domesticity.

▩ *Today, African-Americans still "jump the broom" into marriage.*

reception entertainment

◉ RECEPTION DANCING All join the traditional <u>tarantella</u> (Italian); <u>horah</u> (Israeli), <u>merengue</u> (Latino). Polish guests pay for a Dollar Dance with the bride. During the Cajun broom dance, older unwed siblings dance alone with a decorated broom to playfully mock their single status, while wedding guests pin money to the bride's veil.

◉ WEDDING GAMES In India, where many marriages are arranged, wedding games help break the ice for bashful couples. The winner has the upper hand in marriage. An Italian groom's tie is cut into pieces and sold for honeymoon money. Ukrainians stage a mock capture of the bride; guests encircle the bride until the groom breaks through to claim her.

◉ RECEPTION PICNICS The most popular day for Swedish weddings is Whitsunday, also a traditional day for picnicking. This celebration of spring includes a mock wedding of youths in the church, under a bower of trees and field flowers. Many now carry on the lucky tradition with outdoor wedding celebrations and reception picnics.

▓ *A tree-fastened crystal chandelier (right).*

Favors are mementos given to each guest as a thank-you for sharing your special day. A bit of the bride's good fortune goes home with each. Knotted ribbons, symbolic of tying the knot, are especially propitious. Others: frames for wedding photos, break-away flower centerpieces, small bottles of wine. ❁ Italian receptions end with a second sweet receiving line, at which <u>bomboniere</u>, such as sugared almonds (<u>confetti</u>), heart-shaped cookies, porcelain boxes, net bags, are exchanged.

favors & keepsakes

At this time, guests often give the couple the money envelopes. ❁ Each guest at a Malaysian wedding is given an exquisitely decorated hard-boiled egg, a symbol of fertility. The bride's family spends weeks preparing the eggs and weaving little baskets to hold them.

Diminutive sweets (above); fresh flower petals for tossing (right).

Imaginative creations make memorable favors. Give guests gifts from the garden (seedling packets); the kitchen (tiny cakes with Swiss-dotted and ruffled icing that echoes your gown details). Symbolic of the fruitfulness of life, marzipan and jellied sweets, fashioned like little fruits, can be attached with florist wire to cherry-blossom sprigs — charming favors. Set them at each place or hand them out personally at the wedding's end.

⚬ THE GUEST BOOK Years from now, this permanent written reminder of all who shared in your wedding day will bring back cherished memories. Have one made in leather or tapestry, or create your own with lace and ribbon, handmade paper, or pressed flowers. Decorate a small table for the guest book with memento photos, flowers, and seat an elderly relative there to encourage all guests to sign. Perhaps a special friend might circulate the book during the reception. With indelible ink, guests can also sign a Wedding Cloth, created just for the occasion.

Favorable choices: Top: (left) Small, fresh herbal wreaths of fragrant myrtle, for innocence; (right) monogrammed mints in a porcelain keepsake cup. Bottom: (left) Hearts and flowers—sweet minicakes; (right) a sweet favor for a spring wedding.

reception tosses

❋ FRAGRANT FLOWERS
The bride was imbued with the
power to transmit good fortune.
Hoping for a bit of luck, spec-
tators in early England tore away
bits of her clothing and grabbed for
her fortuitous flowers, ribbons, and
headdress. In self-defense, she
tossed her bouquet. Today, the
single woman who catches it will
marry next.

❋ ALL FOR PROSPERITY The nuptial pair run
through a shower of rice, confetti, birdseed, potpourri,
rose petals ... and in Iraq, chocolate! All are a generous
wish for a fruitful, plentiful married life.

❋ GARTER GAMES The garter is a vestigial acces-
sory in the age of pantyhose. The bride usually wears a
frilly white-on-blue leg band anyway so single men can
also share a bit of luck. In bawdier times, the garter was
snatched away during the ceremony and worn as a prize.

new beginnings

⚙ GRAND EXITS
English couples —
from royals to com-
moners — exit with old
shoes tied to the back of the wedding car, or with satin
slippers tossed after them. Shoes represent a transfer of
property from father to groom.

Today's horn-honking post-wedding parade has its
roots in defending the innocent maiden. Traveling on foot,
or in an open carriage, the bride was an easy target for evil
spirits. Defenders frightened them away with firecrackers

and bells. Novel transport, such as a helicopter, canoe, horsedrawn carriage, or bicycle-built-for-two, will make your departure even more exciting.

After Iranian families share tea at the bride's home, newlyweds sit in a decorated car. Only the bride's family says farewell—the bride is now in the groom's family.

◉ THE THRESHOLD

When newlyweds stepped into their new home, evil spirits were thought to lurk beneath the threshold. A gallant groom carried his bride to safety and happiness inside.

Polish parents present newlyweds with a symbolic first meal of salt (tears), bread (work), and wine (joy).

◉ THE HONEYMOON

That month of sweetness was once a time of hiding from families and imbibing mead, a fermented honey. Now honeymoons — from several days to a week or more—are jointly planned escapes before life's real adventure begins.